fast & simple
100 everyday recipes

First published in 2011
LOVE FOOD is an imprint of Parragon Books Ltd

Parragon
Queen Street House
4 Queen Street
Bath BA1 1HE, UK

ISBN: 978-1-4454-4715-5

Printed in China

Produced by Ivy Contract
Cover photography by Mike Cooper
Cover image home economy and food styling by Lincoln Jefferson

Notes for the Reader

This book uses imperial, metric, and US cup measurements. Follow the same units of measurement throughout; do not mix imperial and metric. All spoon measurements are level: teaspoons are assumed to be 5 ml, and tablespoons are assumed to be 15 ml. Unless otherwise stated, milk is assumed to be whole, eggs and individual vegetables, such as potatoes, are medium, and pepper is freshly ground black pepper.

The times given are an approximate guide only. Preparation times differ according to the techniques used by different people and the cooking times may also vary from those given as a result of the type of oven used. Optional ingredients, variations, or serving suggestions have not been included in the calculations.

Recipes using raw or very lightly cooked eggs should be avoided by infants, the elderly, pregnant women, convalescents, and anyone with a chronic condition. Pregnant and breast-feeding women are advised to avoid eating peanuts and peanut products. People with nut allergies should be aware that some of the prepared ingredients used in the recipes in this book may contain nuts. Always check the package before use.

Vegetarians should be aware that some of the ready-made ingredients used in the recipes in this book may contain animal products. Always check the packaging before use.

fast & simple

introduction

If you don't have the time or the inclination to spend a lot of time in the kitchen, but enjoy fresh, tas[ty] wholesome food and creative cooking, then these recipes are for you. Most of the recipes take just te[n] minutes (or less) to make. They are full of flavor and goodness, but take little time and effort, as the food [is] prepared and cooked very quickly.

Convenience foods and ready meals are expensive, often boring, and usually have a bland [or] "artificial" flavor designed to appeal to a mass market. More importantly they are frequently loaded wi[th] preservatives to give them a longer shelf life. But "fast" food doesn't have to mean a cocktail of nas[ty] chemicals. You can cook fresh meals quickly with minimum fuss but maximum flavor and, of course, you[u] know exactly what has gone into them.

The keys to success are using top quality foods; always choose the freshest and best quality produ[ce] for optimum flavor, such as free-range eggs, vibrant fruit and vegetables free from blemishes and bruise[s], fresh herbs, extra virgin olive oil, and so on. A well-stocked pantry and good utensils make cooking muc[h]

asier, and basic staples should include rice and pasta. Both fresh and dried pasta come in a variety of hapes and sizes, and cook in minutes. Good seasoning is particularly important when food is cooked or a short time, so a stock of good wine vinegar, honey, spices, herbs, and sauces, such as Tabasco and Worcestershire are invaluable to use in recipes to add interest and variety. Canned fish (sardines, anchovies, una), tomatoes, corn, and beans are also excellent to keep in the cupboard and you can use these old avorites to add a new imaginative twist to recipes. Cream and yogurt are wonderfully versatile ingredients, erfect for pouring, whisking, and spooning, and will add a richness to sweet and savory dishes. In the reezer, ready-rolled pie dough and good quality ice cream are ideal standbys.

There's no fiddly preparation in any of these recipes—no elaborate trimmings, fancy decorations or arnishes—just simple food that looks and tastes fabulous. There is nothing better or more delicious than naking your own meals, so try these trouble-free, straightforward recipes and taste the difference.

under 10 minutes

garden pea soup

ingredients

serves 1

2½ cups vegetable stock
1 lb/450 g fresh peas
pinch of granulated sugar
½ cup light cream
salt and pepper
2 tbsp light cream, to garnish
4 crusty rolls, to serve

method

1 Bring the stock to a boil in a large pan. Add the peas and cook for 5 minutes.

2 Remove the pan from the heat, season with salt and pepper, and sugar, then transfer to a food processor and process until smooth.

3 Pour into a pan, stir in the cream, and heat gently to simmering point.

4 Taste and adjust the seasoning if necessary, then pour into 4 serving bowls, adding a swirl of light cream to each bowl. Serve with crusty rolls.

chilled avocado soup

ingredients

serves 6

4 ripe avocados, halved,
    stoned and peeled
1 garlic clove
5 cups vegetable stock
4 tbsp lime juice
pinch of cayenne pepper
salt and pepper
2 tbsp snipped chives,
    to garnish
French bread, to serve

method

1 Put the avocados, garlic, stock, lime juice and cayenne
    pepper into a food processor or blender and process
    until the soup is smooth.

2 Season with salt and pepper to taste and leave to
    chill in the refrigerator until ready to serve. Pour into
    4 chilled bowls, garnish with chives and serve with
    French bread.

hummus with crudités

ingredients

serves 4

6 oz/175 g canned chickpeas
½ cup tahini
2 garlic cloves
½ cup lemon juice
2–3 tbsp water
1 tbsp olive oil
1 tbsp chopped fresh parsley
pinch of cayenne pepper
salt

crudités

selection of vegetables, including
    carrots, cauliflower, and celery

method

1 Drain and rinse the chickpeas. Place them in a blender or food processor with the tahini, garlic, and lemon juice and season to taste with salt. Process, gradually adding the water, until smooth and creamy.

2 Scrape the chickpea mixture into a serving bowl and make a hollow in the center. Pour the olive oil into the hollow and sprinkle with the chopped fresh parsley and the cayenne pepper.

3 Slice the raw vegetables into bite-size portions and arrange on a large serving platter. Serve with the bowl of hummus.

prosciutto & figs

ingredients

serves 4

12 oz/350 g prosciutto
    di Parma, thinly sliced
8 fresh figs
pepper

method

1 Using a sharp knife, trim the visible fat from the slices of prosciutto and discard. Arrange the prosciutto on 4 large serving plates, loosely folding it so that it falls into decorative shapes. Season to taste with pepper.

2 Cut each fig downwards into quarters from the stalk end, but without cutting all the way through. Gently open out each fruit like a flower and place 2 on each of the 4 large serving plates. Season to taste with pepper and serve at room temperature.

three-color salad

ingredients

serves 4

10 oz/280 g buffalo mozzarella,
    drained and thinly sliced
8 tomatoes, sliced
20 fresh basil leaves
½ cup extra virgin olive oil
salt and pepper

method

1 Arrange the mozzarella cheese and tomato slices on 4 individual serving plates and season to taste with salt. Set aside in a cool place for 30 minutes.

2 Sprinkle the basil leaves over the salad and drizzle with the olive oil. Season with pepper and serve immediately.

ham & cheese croissant

ingredients

serves 1

1 croissant
1 egg, hard-cooked and sliced
2 thin slices cooked ham, halved
mustard (optional)
2 slices cheddar cheese

method

1 Preheat the broiler to medium–high. Slice the croissant horizontally in half, then lay it, cut sides up, on the rack in the broiler pan.

2 Top the croissant with the hard-cooked egg and slices of ham, and spread with a little mustard, if using. Then top with the cheese, cutting and overlapping the slices to fit the croissant. Cook for about 2 minutes under the preheated broiler, until the cheese has melted. The croissant will be warmed through and beginning to brown around the edges.

3 Invert the top half of the croissant on top of the bottom half. Serve immediately.

spiced scrambled eggs

ingredients

serves 2

4 eggs
²/₃ cup light cream
pinch of saffron
2 tbsp butter
½ tsp ground cumin
½–1 tsp harissa paste
1 tsp ground coriander
salt and pepper
2 slices of freshly toasted bread,
    buttered if wanted, to serve

method

1 Whisk the eggs, cream, salt and pepper, and saffron together in a bowl.

2 Melt the butter in a skillet and add the cumin, harissa and ground coriander. Cook gently for 1 minute.

3 Pour in the egg mixture and cook, stirring, for a few minutes until the eggs are just set. Serve the spiced scrambled eggs on top of the freshly toasted bread.

pear & blue cheese open sandwiches

ingredients

serves 2–4

4 slices walnut bread,
 about ½ inch/1 cm thick
4 thin slices prosciutto
2 ripe pears, such as Conference,
 peeled, halved, cored, and
 thinly sliced lengthwise
3½ oz/100 g blue cheese, very
 thinly sliced

method

1 Preheat the broiler to medium–high. Toast the bread slices on both sides until crisp but not brown. Do not turn off the broiler.

2 Fold or cut the prosciutto slices to cover each slice of bread, then divide the pear slices equally between the bread slices. Lay the cheese slices on top.

3 Return the bread slices to the broiler and cook until the cheese melts and bubbles. Serve immediately.

smoked trout with pears

ingredients

serves 4

1¼ cups watercress or arugula
1 head of radicchio, torn into pieces
4 smoked trout fillets, skinned
2 ripe pears, such as Bartlett
2 tbsp lemon juice
2 tbsp extra virgin olive oil
3 tbsp sour cream
2 tsp creamed horseradish
salt and pepper
thinly sliced whole wheat bread,
    buttered, to serve

method

1 Place the watercress and radicchio in a bowl. Cut the trout fillets into thin strips and add to the bowl. Halve and core the pears, then slice thinly. Place in a separate bowl, add 4 teaspoons of the lemon juice, and toss to coat. Add the pears to the salad.

2 To make the dressing, mix the remaining lemon juice and the olive oil together in a bowl, then season to taste with salt and pepper. Pour the dressing over the salad and toss well. Transfer to a large salad bowl.

3 Mix the sour cream and horseradish together in a separate bowl until thoroughly blended and pour into a small serving bowl. Serve the salad with the horseradish cream and buttered whole wheat bread.

warm goat cheese salad

ingredients

serves 4

1 small iceberg lettuce,
    torn into pieces
handful of arugula leaves
few radicchio leaves, torn
6 slices French bread
4 oz/115 g goat cheese, sliced

dressing

4 tbsp extra virgin olive oil
1 tbsp white wine vinegar
salt and pepper

method

1 Divide all the leaves among 4 individual salad bowls.

2 Preheat the broiler. Toast one side of the bread under the broiler until golden. Place a slice of cheese on top of each untoasted side and toast until the cheese is just melting.

3 Put all the dressing ingredients into a bowl and beat together until combined. Pour over the leaves, tossing to coat.

4 Cut each slice of bread in half and place 3 halves on top of each salad. Toss very gently to combine and serve warm.

tagliatelle with lemon & thyme

ingredients

serves 2-4

12 oz/350 g fresh tagliatelle
6 tbsp butter
finely grated zest and juice
    of 1 lemon
salt and pepper
2 tbsp chopped fresh thyme,
    plus extra sprigs to garnish

method

1 Cook the pasta in a large pan of boiling salted water for about 4 minutes, or according to the package directions, until tender but still firm to the bite.

2 Drain the pasta, keeping about 3 tablespoons of the cooking liquid in it. Stir in the butter, grated lemon zest and lemon juice, thyme, and salt and pepper, and toss well to mix. Serve immediately, garnished with the thyme sprigs.

creamy ricotta, mint & garlic pasta

ingredients

serves 4

10½ oz/300 g short fresh
    pasta shapes
heaping ½ cup ricotta cheese
1–2 roasted garlic cloves from
    a jar, finely chopped
⅔ cup heavy cream
salt and pepper
1 tbsp chopped fresh mint,
    plus extra to garnish

method

1 Cook the pasta in a large pan of boiling salted water
    for about 3 minutes, or according to the package
    directions until tender but still firm to the bite.

2 Beat the ricotta, garlic, cream, and chopped mint
    together in a bowl until smooth.

3 Drain the cooked pasta then tip back into the pan.
    Pour in the cheese mixture and toss together.

4 Season with pepper and serve immediately, garnished
    with the sprigs of mint.

microwave herbed fish pockets

ingredients

serves 4

4 firm white fish fillets, such
    as monkfish, about
    4 oz/115 g each
4 tbsp lemon juice
4 tbsp white wine or cider
4 tbsp chopped fresh parsley
4 fresh thyme sprigs
4 fresh rosemary sprigs
4 tomatoes, thinly sliced

method

1 Place a fish fillet in the center of four 12-inch/30-cm
   squares of parchment paper.

2 Sprinkle each fillet with 1 tablespoon of lemon
   juice and 1 tablespoon of white wine, followed by
   1 tablespoon of chopped parsley. Add a sprig of thyme
   and rosemary to each parcel.

3 Arrange the tomatoes over each fillet, overlapping
   them. Fold in the edges of the parchment paper
   squares to completely enclose the filling and form
   pockets. Place the pockets in a circle on a heatproof
   plate, leaving a 1-inch/2.5-cm space between each
   pocket, and cook in the microwave oven on high for
   7 minutes. Serve immediately.

peppered tuna steaks

ingredients

serves 4

4 tuna steaks, about
6 oz/175 g each
4 tsp sunflower or olive oil
1 tsp salt
2 tbsp mixed pink, green, and
black peppercorns, coarsely
crushed

to serve

handful of fresh arugula leaves
lemon wedges
4 baked potatoes (optional)
2 tbsp butter

method

1 Brush the tuna steaks with the oil and sprinkle with sa

2 Coat the tuna in the crushed peppercorns.

3 Meanwhile, heat a ridged grill pan or skillet and,
when hot, add the fish and cook over medium heat
for 2 to 3 minutes on each side. Serve with some
arugula leaves, lemon wedges on the side and baked
potatoes with butter, if using.

strawberry & banana parfait

ingredients

serves 4–6

4 large bananas
1 lb/450 g strawberries, hulled,
    plus extra whole strawberries,
    to decorate
1¼ cups heavy cream, whipped
granulated or superfine sugar,
    if necessary
cookies, such as cigarettes russes,
    to serve

method

1 Peel the bananas and put in a food processor with the strawberries. Process to a smooth purée and tip into a large bowl.

2 Gently stir in the whipped cream. Sweeten to taste if needed and spoon into serving glasses.

3 Chill in the refrigerator until you are ready to serve. Decorate with a whole strawberry and serve with light crunchy cookies.

french toast with maple syrup

ingredients

serves 4-6

6 eggs
¾ cup milk
¼ tsp ground cinnamon
12 slices day-old plain white
    bread
about 4 tbsp butter or margarine,
    plus extra to serve
½–1 tbsp sunflower or corn oil
salt
warm maple syrup, to serve

method

1 Preheat the oven to 275°F/140°C.

2 Break the eggs into a large, shallow bowl and beat together with the milk, cinnamon, and salt to taste. Add the bread slices and press them down so that they are covered on both sides with the egg mixture. Let the bread stand for 1–2 minutes to soak up the egg mixture, turning the slices over once.

3 Melt half the butter with ½ tablespoon of oil in a large skillet. Add to the pan as many bread slices as will fit in a single layer and cook for 2–3 minutes, until golden brown.

4 Turn the bread slices over and cook until golden brown on the other side. Transfer the French toast to a plate and keep warm in the oven while cooking the remaining bread slices, adding extra oil to the pan if necessary.

5 Serve the French toast with some butter melting on top and warm maple syrup for pouring over.

broiled cinnamon oranges

ingredients

serves 4

2 large oranges
1 tsp ground cinnamon
1 tbsp raw brown sugar

method

1 Cut the oranges in half and discard any seeds. Using a sharp or curved grapefruit knife, carefully cut the flesh away from the skin by cutting around the edge of the fruit. Cut across the segments to loosen the flesh into bite-size pieces that will then spoon out easily.

2 Arrange the orange halves, cut-side up, in a shallow, flameproof dish. Mix the cinnamon with the sugar in a small bowl and sprinkle evenly over the orange halves

3 Preheat the broiler to high. Broil for 3–5 minutes, or until the sugar has caramelized and is golden and bubbling. Serve immediately.

variation

Substitute 2 white grapefruits for the oranges. Drizzle each half with 1 teaspoon of honey and sprinkle with cinnamon, omitting the sugar, before broiling.

meat & poultry

farfalle with blue cheese & ham

ingredients

serves 4

1 cup sour cream
8 oz/225 g cremini mushrooms,
    quartered
14 oz/400 g dried farfalle
3 oz/85 g blue cheese, crumbled
1 tbsp chopped fresh flat-leaf
    parsley, plus extra sprigs to
    garnish
1 cup diced cooked ham
salt and pepper

method

1 Pour the sour cream into a pan, add the mushrooms, and season to taste with salt and pepper. Bring to just below the boil, then lower the heat, and simmer very gently, stirring occasionally, until the sauce has thickened.

2 Meanwhile, bring a large pan of lightly salted water to a boil. Add the pasta, bring back to a boil, and cook for 8–10 minutes, until tender but still firm to the bite.

3 Remove the pan of mushrooms from the heat and stir in the blue cheese until it has melted. Return the pan to a very low heat and stir in the chopped parsley and ham.

4 Drain the pasta and add it to the sauce. Toss lightly, then divide among individual warmed dishes, garnish with the parsley sprigs, and serve.

spaghetti carbonara

ingredients

serves 4

1 lb/450 g fresh spaghetti
2 tbsp butter
6 slices bacon, diced
3 eggs
2 tbsp light cream
4 tbsp freshly grated
    Parmesan cheese
salt and pepper
chopped fresh parsley,
    for garnish

method

1 Cook the spaghetti in a large pan of boiling salted water for about 2–4 minutes, or according to the package directions, until tender but still firm to the bi

2 Meanwhile, heat the butter in a skillet, add the bacon and cook until crisp. Keep warm.

3 Beat the eggs, cream, and cheese together in a bowl and season with salt and pepper.

4 As soon as the spaghetti is cooked, drain and return to the pan over low heat.

5 Add the bacon, and egg and cream mixture, and quickly toss the spaghetti several times until the sauc begins to thicken and the spaghetti is coated. Serve immediately garnished with chopped parsley.

spinach & ham casserole

ingredients

serves 2

good handful of fresh baby
    spinach leaves
4 slices ham
4 eggs
4 tbsp heavy cream
½ cup grated cheese, such
    as Gruyère or cheddar
salt and pepper

method

1 Put the spinach in a large bowl and pour boiling water
    over it. Let stand until the leaves are wilted, then drain
    well on paper towels.

2 Preheat the broiler. Line 2 small ovenproof dishes with
    the ham, it doesn't matter if the slices overlap the
    edges, and spread the drained spinach evenly over
    the top. Season well with salt and pepper.

3 Break in the eggs and drizzle over the cream. Sprinkle
    with the cheese and broil for 8 to 10 minutes, or until
    the eggs are cooked to your liking and the cheese is
    bubbling.

sweet & sour pork

ingredients

serves 4

1 tbsp vegetable oil
12 oz/350 g lean pork, cut
    into ¼-inch/5-mm strips
1 large red bell pepper,
    seeded and sliced
4 scallions, trimmed
    and chopped, plus extra
    to garnish
1 lb/450 g canned pineapple
    pieces in juice
2 tbsp cornstarch
3 tbsp wine vinegar
juice of 1 lemon
3 tbsp light soy sauce
2 tbsp granulated sugar
salt and pepper

method

1 Heat the oil in a large skillet, add the pork strips, and cook for 5 minutes, stirring.

2 Add the red bell pepper and scallions to the skillet and cook for 3 minutes, stirring until they begin to soften.

3 Drain the pineapple juice into a bowl, reserving the pineapple pieces, and whisk in the cornstarch, vinegar, lemon juice, soy sauce, sugar and salt and pepper.

4 Add the mixture to the skillet and cook over medium heat for 1–2 minutes, stirring until slightly thickened. Add the reserved pineapple pieces and heat through for 1 minute. Serve immediately, garnished with scallions.

spicy pork meatballs

ingredients

serves 4

1 lb 8 oz/675 g fresh lean
ground pork
1 garlic clove, finely chopped
1 tsp ground ginger
pinch of ground cloves
½ tsp freshly grated nutmeg
½ tsp ground allspice
½ tsp salt
½ tsp black pepper
2 egg yolks
¼ cup ground almonds
2–3 tbsp sunflower or olive oil

method

1 Mix the ground pork, garlic, spices, salt, pepper, egg
yolks, and ground almonds together in a large bowl.
Form into balls and brush with the oil.

2 Preheat the broiler to medium–high. Broil the
meatballs, turning from time to time for about
8–10 minutes, or until cooked through.

3 Alternatively, heat the oil in a large skillet and pan-fry
the meatballs for about 8–10 minutes, or until cooked
through. Serve immediately.

stir-fried ginger pork

ingredients

serves 2

2 tbsp sunflower or olive oil
½-inch/1-cm piece fresh ginger,
    peeled and grated
1 garlic clove, crushed
2 boneless pork steaks,
    cut into thin strips
3 oz/85 g shredded white cabbage
4 tbsp cashew nuts
2 tbsp dark soy sauce
1 tbsp dry white wine
1 tsp granulated sugar
1 tsp sesame oil
salt and pepper

method

1 Heat a wok over high heat and when smoking, add
   1 tablespoon of oil, swirling it around the wok.

2 Add the ginger and garlic and cook quickly for
   20 seconds. Add the pork and cook for 3–4 minutes,
   or until just cooked through. Remove the pork, ginger
   and garlic from the wok and keep warm.

3 Add the remaining oil to the wok and when hot add
   the cabbage, and cook for 2–3 minutes until tender.
   Add the cashew nuts and cook for 3 seconds.

4 Return the pork, ginger, and garlic to the wok with
   the soy sauce, wine, and sugar. Cook for 1 minute the
   add the sesame oil and season with salt and pepper.
   Serve immediately.

orange & lemon-coated crispy lamb cutlets

ingredients

serves 2

1 garlic clove, crushed

1 tbsp olive oil

2 tbsp finely grated orange zest

2 tbsp finely grated lemon zest

6 lamb chops

salt and pepper

orange wedges, to garnish

method

1 Mix the garlic, oil, grated orange zest and lemon zest, and salt and pepper together in a bowl.

2 Preheat the broiler to medium–high. Brush the mixture over the lamb chops and broil for 4–5 minutes on each side. Serve, garnished with the orange wedges.

hamburgers

ingredients

serves 4

1 lb 7 oz/650 g fresh ground beef
1 red bell pepper, seeded and
    finely chopped
1 garlic clove, finely chopped
2 small red chiles, seeded and
    finely chopped
1 tbsp chopped fresh basil
½ tsp ground cumin
salt and pepper
sprigs of fresh basil, to garnish
hamburger buns, to serve

method

1 Put the ground beef, red bell pepper, garlic, chiles, chopped basil, and cumin into a bowl and mix until well combined. Season with salt and pepper. Using your hands, form the mixture into burger shapes.

2 Preheat the broiler to medium–high. Cook the burger over hot coals or broil for 5–8 minutes on each side, or until cooked through. Garnish with sprigs of basil and serve in hamburger buns.

teriyaki steak

ingredients

serves 4

4 beef steaks, about
    5½ oz/150 g each
2 tbsp vegetable oil
heaping 1¼ cups bean
    sprouts, trimmed
4 scallions, trimmed
    and finely sliced
salt and pepper

teriyaki sauce

2 tbsp mirin (Japanese rice wine)
2 tbsp sake or pale dry sherry
4 tbsp dark soy sauce
1 tsp granulated or superfine
    sugar

method

1 Season the steaks with salt and pepper and set aside.

2 To make the sauce, combine the mirin, sake, soy sauce and sugar in a bowl, stirring well.

3 Heat 1 tablespoon of oil in a skillet over high heat. Add the bean sprouts and sauté quickly, tossing them in the hot oil for 30 seconds. Remove from the skillet and drain on paper towels.

4 Add the remaining oil to the skillet and when hot add the steaks. Cook for 1–3 minutes on each side, according to how rare you like your meat. Remove from the skillet and keep warm.

5 Remove the skillet from the heat and add the sauce and scallions. Return to the heat and simmer for 2 minutes, stirring until the sauce thickens slightly and is glossy.

6 Slice each steak and arrange on a bed of bean sprouts. Spoon over the sauce and serve immediately.

stir-fried beef with cashew nuts

ingredients

serves 2

2 tbsp sunflower or olive oil
1 lb/450 g top round steak,
    cut into thin strips
1 tbsp black peppercorns, crushed
2 fresh chiles, seeded
    and finely chopped
bunch of scallions, trimmed and
    thinly sliced or chopped
¾ cup cashew nuts

sauce

3 tbsp soy sauce
2 tbsp rice wine or dry sherry
1 tbsp dark brown sugar
1 tsp five spice powder

method

1 Heat the oil in a preheated wok until smoking. Add
    the steak strips, crushed peppercorns, chiles, and
    scallions and cook for 3–4 minutes, tossing the wok
    to cook evenly.

2 Mix all the ingredients for the sauce together in a bowl
    and pour into the wok. Cook for 3 minutes, tossing the
    ingredients until everything is heated through.

3 Add the cashew nuts and toss to combine. Serve the
    stir-fry immediately.

peppered steaks in whisky cream sauce

ingredients

serves 4

3 tbsp black peppercorns, crushed
4 minute steaks, about
    6 oz/175 g each
2 tbsp sunflower or olive oil
8 baby carrots, freshly cooked
fresh flat-leaf parsley sprigs,
    to garnish

whisky cream sauce

²/₃ cup heavy cream
2 tbsp beef stock
2–3 tbsp malt whisky

method

1 Press the crushed peppercorns firmly into the steaks to coat both sides.

2 Heat the oil in a skillet and when hot, place the steaks in the skillet and cook for 1 minute on each side.

3 Remove the steaks and keep warm. Pour off the oil from the skillet.

4 Mix the cream, stock, whisky, and any juices from the steaks together in a bowl and pour into the skillet. Heat through, stirring, then pour over the steaks. Divide the carrots evenly among 4 warmed plates; add the steaks, garnish with a sprig of parsley, and serve immediately.

beef & blue cheese wraps

ingredients

serves 4

9 oz/250 g beef sirloin steak
1 tbsp olive oil
4½ oz/125 g blue cheese,
    crumbled
1 tbsp mayonnaise
4 x 10-inch/25-cm wraps
a small bunch of fresh
    watercress
salt and pepper

method

1 Season the steak with salt and pepper.

2 Preheat a nonstick skillet until almost smoking. Add t
   oil, then add the steak and seal, cooking for 30 secon
   on each side for very rare (or longer according to
   personal preference). Remove from the skillet and se
   aside to rest for a few minutes. Cut into thin strips wi
   a sharp knife.

3 Mix together the blue cheese and mayonnaise.

4 Preheat a nonstick skillet or broiler pan until almost
   smoking, add the wraps, 1 at a time, and cook for
   10 seconds on each side. This will add some color an
   soften the wraps.

5 Divide the steak between the wraps, placing it along
   the middle of each wrap. Top with the cheese and
   mayonnaise mixture, and then with watercress,
   reserving a little for the garnish. Roll up, cut in half
   and serve, garnished with the remaining watercress.

chicken satay

ingredients

serves 4

4 tbsp smooth peanut butter
generous 1/3 cup soy sauce
4 skinless, boneless chicken
　　breasts, cut into thin strips
freshly cooked rice and lemon
　　wedges, to serve

method

1 Mix the peanut butter and soy sauce together in a bowl until smooth. Stir in the chicken strips, tossing well to coat in the mixture.

2 If you are using wooden skewers, soak them in cold water for at least 30 minutes to prevent them from burning. Thread the chicken strips onto the skewers.

3 Preheat the broiler to high. Broil the skewers for about 5 minutes on each side until cooked through. Serve immediately with rice and lemon wedges.

chicken skewers

ingredients

serves 8

1 lb/450 g ground chicken
1 onion, finely chopped
1 fresh red chile, seeded
    and chopped
2 tbsp Thai red curry paste
1 tsp jaggery or soft light
    brown sugar
1 tsp ground coriander
1 tsp ground cumin
1 egg white
8 lemongrass stalks
sprigs of cilantro, to garnish
boiled rice with chopped scallion,
    to serve

method

1 Combine the chicken, onion, chile, curry paste, and sugar in a bowl and stir well to make a thick paste. Stir in the ground coriander, cumin, and egg white, and mix again.

2 Divide the mixture into 8 equal portions and squeeze them around each of the lemongrass stalks.

3 Preheat the broiler to high. Arrange the skewers on a broiler pan and broil, turning frequently, until browned and cooked through. Garnish with the cilantro sprigs and serve immediately, accompanied by cooked rice and chopped scallion stirred through it.

fragrant chicken

ingredients

serves 4

1 fresh red chile, seeded
    and finely chopped
3 garlic cloves, finely chopped
4 scallions, trimmed and
    finely chopped
½–¾-inch/1–2-cm piece fresh
    ginger, cut into wafer thin slices
1 tsp ground coriander
1 tsp ground cumin
4 tbsp olive oil
4 tbsp pine nuts, lightly crushed
4 skinless, boneless chicken
    breasts, cut into thin slices
1 tbsp chopped fresh cilantro
salt and pepper

method

1 Combine the chile, garlic, scallions, ginger, ground coriander, cumin, 3 tablespoons of oil, and the pine nuts in a bowl and season with salt and pepper.

2 Heat the remaining oil in a wok and, when very hot, add the chicken slices. Cook over high heat for about 4 minutes, or until the chicken is browned all over.

3 Add the chile mixture and cook for 4–5 minutes, or until the chicken is completely cooked.

4 Stir in the fresh cilantro and serve immediately.

chicken with creamy penne

ingredients

serves 2

7 oz/200 g fresh penne pasta
1 tbsp olive oil
2 skinless, boneless chicken breasts
4 tbsp dry white wine
heaping 1 cup frozen peas
5 tbsp heavy cream
salt
4–5 tbsp chopped fresh
    parsley, for garnish

method

1 Cook the penne in a large pan of boiling salted water for about 3–4 minutes, or according to the package directions, until tender but still firm to the bite.

2 Meanwhile, heat the oil in a skillet, add the chicken breasts, and cook over medium heat for about 4 minutes on each side.

3 Pour in the wine and cook over high heat until it has almost evaporated.

4 Drain the pasta. Add the peas, cream, and pasta to the chicken breasts in the skillet and stir well. Cover and simmer for 2 minutes. Serve immediately garnished with chopped parsley.

duck breasts with citrus glaze

ingredients

serves 4

¼ cup light brown sugar,
    plus extra if needed
finely grated zest and juice
    of 1 orange
finely grated zest and juice
    of 1 large lemon
finely grated zest and juice
    of 1 lime
4 duck breasts, skin on
2 tbsp olive oil
salt and pepper
sugar snap peas and orange
    wedges, to serve

method

1 Put the sugar in a small pan, add just enough water to cover, and heat gently until dissolved.

2 Add the citrus zests and juices and bring to a boil. Reduce the heat and simmer for about 10 minutes until the zest is soft, and the liquid is syrupy. Remove the pan from the heat. Taste and add a little more sugar if necessary.

3 Meanwhile, score the skin of the duck breasts with a sharp knife in a criss-cross pattern and season with salt and pepper.

4 Heat the oil in a skillet. Place the duck breasts skin-side up in the skillet and cook for 5 minutes on each side until the flesh is just pink. Keep warm.

5 Slice the duck breasts diagonally into 5–6 slices and arrange on warmed plates.

6 Arrange the sugar snap peas and orange wedges on each plate, spoon over the glaze, and serve immediately.

honeyed duck stir-fry

ingredients

serves 4

2 tbsp honey

4 tbsp soy sauce

4 skinless duck breasts, sliced

1 tbsp olive oil

bunch of scallions,
    trimmed and sliced

1 small head Chinese cabbage,
    finely shredded

salt and pepper

method

1 Mix the honey and soy sauce together in a large bowl.
  Add the duck slices and toss to coat in the mixture.

2 Heat the oil in a wok or skillet. Add the duck strips
  (set aside the honey mixture) and cook quickly for
  2 minutes until browned.

3 Add the scallions, Chinese cabbage, and the reserved
  honey mixture. Cook for 3–4 minutes until the duck is
  cooked but still a little pink in the center.

4 Season with salt and pepper and serve immediately.

turkey sandwich with walnuts

ingredients

serves 2

2 ciabatta rolls
4 oz/115 g blue cheese, such as
    Stilton or Danish blue, finely
    diced or crumbled
¾ cup walnuts, chopped
8 large fresh sage leaves,
    finely shredded
4 slices cooked turkey breast
seedless green grapes, to serve

method

1 Preheat the broiler to medium–high. Slice the ciabatta rolls in half horizontally and toast the cut sides under the broiler. Remove the top halves. Turn the bottom halves over and toast the undersides until brown and crisp. When the breads are toasted, set them aside and reduce the heat to a low setting.

2 Meanwhile, mix together the blue cheese, walnuts, and sage. Lay 2 turkey slices on the base of each roll and top with the cheese and walnut mixture, piling it up in the middle. Cover with the top of the roll.

3 Heat the rolls under the preheated broiler, well away from the heat, for 3–4 minutes, until the bread is hot, and the cheese is beginning to melt. Increase the heat slightly, if necessary, to a medium setting, but do not turn it up high enough to brown the tops of the rolls before they are warmed through.

4 Serve the hot turkey rolls with some green grapes.

fish & seafood

garlic-sizzled shrimp with chili dipping sauce

ingredients

serves 3–4

2 tbsp sunflower or olive oil
1–2 garlic cloves, crushed
bunch of scallions,
    trimmed and chopped
12 oz/350 g raw peeled shrimp,
    with tails left on
chopped fresh chives, to garnish
lime wedges, to serve

chili dipping sauce

2 tbsp molasses
6 tbsp white wine vinegar
2 tbsp Thai fish sauce or
    light soy sauce
2 tbsp water
1 garlic clove, crushed
2 tsp grated fresh ginger
2 tsp finely chopped, seeded
    fresh red chile

method

1 To make the sauce, heat the molasses, vinegar, fish sauce, and water in a small pan until boiling. Add the garlic, ginger, and chile and pour the sauce into a sm serving bowl.

2 Heat the oil in a wok or skillet and add the garlic and scallions. Cook over high heat for 2 minutes then add the shrimp, stir-frying them for 2–3 minutes until cooked.

3 Divide between 4 warmed serving plates. Garnish with chives and serve with lime wedges and the chi dipping sauce.

hot & sour shrimp soup

ingredients

serves 2

10½ oz/300 g raw peeled shrimp
2 tsp vegetable oil
2 fresh red chiles, sliced
1 garlic clove, sliced
about 3 cups fish stock
4 thin slices fresh ginger
2 lemongrass stalks, bruised
5 Thai lime leaves, shredded
2 tsp jaggery or brown sugar
1 tbsp chili oil
handful of fresh cilantro leaves
dash of lime juice

method

1 Dry-fry the shrimp in a skillet or wok until they turn pink. Remove and set aside.

2 Heat the vegetable oil in the same skillet, add the chi and garlic and cook for 30 seconds.

3 Add the stock, ginger, lemongrass, Thai lime leaves, and sugar and simmer for 4 minutes. Add the reserve shrimp with the chili oil, and cilantro and cook for 1–2 minutes.

4 Stir in the lime juice and serve immediately.

shrimp toasts

ingredients

serves 2–4

3½ oz/100 g shelled and
    deveined raw shrimp
2 egg whites
2 tbsp cornstarch
½ tsp sugar
pinch of salt
2 tbsp finely chopped fresh
    cilantro leaves
2 slices day-old white bread
vegetable or peanut oil,
    for deep-frying

method

1 Pound the shrimp to a pulp in a mortar with a pestle
   or with the bottom of a cleaver.

2 Mix the shrimp with one of the egg whites and half
   the cornstarch in a bowl. Add the sugar and salt, and
   stir in the cilantro. Mix the remaining egg white with
   the remaining cornstarch in a pitcher.

3 Remove the crusts from the bread and cut each
   slice into 8 triangles. Brush the top of each piece with
   the egg white and cornstarch mixture, then add
   1 teaspoon of the shrimp mixture and spread smooth
   over the top.

4 Heat enough oil for deep-frying in a wok, deep-fat
   fryer, or large, heavy pan until it reaches 350°F/180°C,
   or until a cube of bread browns in 30 seconds. Without
   overcrowding the wok, cook the toasts shrimp-side
   up for 2 minutes. Turn and cook for an additional
   2 minutes, or until beginning to turn golden brown.
   Remove with a slotted spoon, then drain on paper
   towels and keep warm in a low oven while cooking
   the remainder before serving.

pancetta-wrapped scallops

ingredients

serves 4

16 large fresh scallops
8 slices pancetta, halved
1 tbsp olive oil
juice of 1 lemon
pepper
lemon wedges, to serve

method

1 Wrap each scallop in half a slice of pancetta.

2 Mix the oil, lemon juice, and a sprinkling of black pepper together in a bowl.

3 Coat the wrapped scallops in the mixture and thread onto metal skewers (4 on each skewer). Discard any leftover lemon juice mixture.

4 Preheat the broiler to medium–hot. Broil the wrapped scallops for 4 to 5 minutes, turning once until cooked. Serve immediately, with lemon wedges.

poached scallops with sweet dill dressing

ingredients

serves 4

12 fresh queen scallops
    with their corals
finely grated rind and juice
    of 2 limes
²⁄₃ cup dry white wine
bunch of scallions, trimmed
    and diagonally sliced
2 tbsp granulated sugar
4 tbsp butter
2 tbsp chopped fresh dill
salt and pepper
fresh dill sprigs and lime slices,
    to garnish

method

1 Put the scallops in a shallow dish. Mix the lime rind, juice, wine, scallions, salt and pepper, and sugar together in a bowl. Pour the mixture over the scallops and turn them to coat well.

2 Heat the butter in a skillet. Using a slotted spoon, remove the scallops from the lime mixture and add to the skillet. Set aside the lime juice mixture. Pan-fry for 2 minutes on each side until almost tender.

3 Stir the lime juice mixture and chopped dill into the skillet. Bring to a boil and boil rapidly for 8 minutes until reduced.

4 Serve immediately, garnished with dill sprigs and lime slices.

oysters au gratin

ingredients

serves 2

4 oz/115 g pancetta
    or bacon, diced
1 oz/25 g celery, finely chopped
4 asparagus tips, finely chopped
6 fresh oysters, shucked
1 oz/25 g firm mozzarella cheese,
    grated
salt and pepper

method

1 Cook the pancetta in a small skillet for 1 to 2 minutes
    until crisp. Add the celery and asparagus and season
    with salt and pepper to taste.

2 Spoon the pancetta and asparagus mixture over the
    oysters. Sprinkle over the grated cheese.

3 Preheat the broiler to medium–hot. Broil the oysters
    for 3 to 4 minutes, or until the cheese is golden brow
    and melted. Serve immediately.

wine-steamed mussels

ingredients

serves 4

½ cup butter
1 shallot, chopped
3 garlic cloves, finely chopped
4½ lb/2 kg live mussels, scrubbed
and beards removed
1 cup dry white wine
½ tsp salt
4 tbsp chopped fresh parsley
pepper

method

1 Melt half the butter in a very large pan over low heat.
Add the shallot and garlic and cook for 2 minutes. Add
the mussels, discarding any with broken shells or any
that refuse to close when tapped, wine, salt, and a
sprinkling of pepper.

2 Cover, bring to a boil, then boil for 3 minutes, shaking
the pan from time to time.

3 Remove the mussels from the pan with a slotted
spoon and place in individual serving bowls. Discard
any mussels that haven't opened.

4 Mix the remaining butter with the parsley in a small
bowl and stir the mixture into the cooking juices in
the pan. Bring to a boil and pour over the mussels.
Serve immediately.

crab wraps

ingredients

serves 4

8 oz/225 g baby fennel
5½ oz/150 g fresh or canned
    white crabmeat
4 tbsp mayonnaise
grated rind and juice of 1 lemon
a small bunch of fresh
    flat-leaf parsley, shredded
4 x 10-inch/25-cm
    Mediterranean herb wraps
salt and pepper

method

1 Cut the fennel in half lengthwise and then slice as thinly as possible.

2 Place the sliced fennel in a bowl with the crabmeat, mayonnaise, salt and pepper, lemon rind and juice, and parsley. Mix well.

3 Set aside for 5 minutes to let the lemon juice wilt the fennel slightly.

4 Preheat a nonstick skillet or broiler pan until almost smoking, add the wraps, one at a time, and cook for 10 seconds on each side. This will add some color and soften the wraps.

5 Stir the filling mixture once and then divide it evenly among the wraps, placing some in the center of each wrap. Fold in each wrap at the ends, roll up, cut in half diagonally, and serve.

crab fritters with avocado salsa

ingredients

serves 4

1¼ cups lightly cooked
    corn kernels
½ cup all-purpose flour
2 eggs, beaten
10½ oz/300 g fresh or canned
    white crabmeat
1 small bunch fresh parsley,
    chopped
3–4 tbsp olive oil
salt and pepper
lime wedges, to serve

avocado salsa

1 small red onion, finely chopped
1 red bell pepper, seeded
    and diced
1 yellow bell pepper, seeded
    and diced
1 avocado, stoned and diced
1 mango, stoned and diced
4 tomatoes, diced
finely grated rind and juice
    of 2 limes
1 large bunch fresh cilantro,
    chopped
salt and pepper

method

1 First make the salsa. Put the onion in a bowl. Add the
   bell peppers. Add the avocado and mango to the bc
   then add the tomatoes. Stir in the lime rind and juice
   and cilantro. Season to taste with salt and pepper.

2 Put the corn kernels, flour, and eggs in a separate bc
   and stir until well mixed. Lightly fold in the crabmea
   and parsley, and season to taste with salt and peppe

3 Heat the oil in a large skillet over medium-high heat
   Drop spoonfuls of the batter into the hot oil and coc
   in batches for 2–3 minutes on each side, until crisp a
   golden. Remove and drain on paper towels. Serve
   immediately with the salsa and the lime wedges.

salmon with lemon & olive dressing

ingredients

serves 4

2 tbsp olive oil
4 salmon fillets, skin on,
    about 6 oz/175 g each
juice of ½ lemon
salt

herb dressing
1 handful fresh basil leaves
2 tbsp snipped fresh chives
1 garlic clove, crushed
1 tsp whole grain mustard
½ tsp superfine sugar
juice of ½ lemon
generous ¾ cup extra virgin
    olive oil
rind of ½ preserved lemon,
    finely chopped
10 pitted black olives,
    finely chopped

method

1 Preheat the oven to 400°F/200°C.

2 To make the dressing, put the herbs, garlic, mustard, sugar, lemon juice, and extra virgin olive oil in a blender or food processor and process until smooth. Pour the mixture into a small saucepan, then add the preserved lemon rind and olives and warm over gentle heat.

3 Meanwhile, heat the olive oil in a skillet over medium heat, then add the salmon fillets, skin-side down, and cook for 3 minutes, or until the skin is golden and crisp. Lay the fish in a roasting pan, skin-side up, then squeeze over the lemon juice and season with a little salt.

4 Roast in the preheated oven for 5 minutes, or until the fish is just cooked through–the exact timing will depend on the thickness of the fillets. Serve immediately with the dressing.

smoked salmon pâté

ingredients

serves 4–6

1 lb/450 g smoked salmon,
    chopped into small pieces
1 tsp chopped fresh thyme
finely grated rind and juice
    of 1 small lemon
2 tbsp soft unsalted butter
1/3 cup soft cream cheese
pinch of paprika
pinch of cayenne pepper
pepper
crispbreads, to serve

method

1 Put the smoked salmon, thyme, lemon rind, and juice in a food processor and process until just combined.

2 Scrape down the sides of the bowl, and add the butter and cheese. Season lightly with the paprika, cayenne, and pepper.

3 Process again until the mixture is blended, but not completely smooth–it should still have a slightly rough texture. Taste the pâté and adjust the seasoning, if necessary.

4 Transfer to an airtight container. Cover with plastic wrap and let chill in the refrigerator until firm. Remove from the refrigerator at least 15 minutes before eating and serve with crispbreads.

smoked salmon tagliatelle

ingredients

serves 4

12 oz/350 g dried tagliatelle
2 tbsp olive oil
1 garlic clove, finely chopped
4 oz/115 g smoked salmon,
    cut into thin strips
1¼ cups arugula
salt and pepper

method

1 Bring a large heavy pan of lightly salted water to a boil. Add the pasta, return to a boil, and cook for 8–10 minutes, or until tender but still firm to the bite.

2 Just before the end of the cooking time, heat the olive oil in a heavy skillet. Add the garlic and cook over low heat, stirring constantly, for 1 minute. Do not let the garlic brown or it will taste bitter.

3 Add the salmon and arugula. Season to taste with pepper and cook, stirring constantly, for 1 minute. Remove the skillet from the heat.

4 Drain the pasta and transfer to a large, warmed serving dish. Add the smoked salmon and arugula mixture, toss lightly, and serve immediately.

variation

For a creamier version of this pasta dish, add 9 oz/250 g plain yogurt, mixed with a squeeze of lemon juice. Replace the arugula with a handful of chopped fresh dill, if preferred.

teriyaki salmon fillets with chinese noodles

ingredients

serves 4

4 salmon fillets,
    about 7 oz/200 g each
½ cup teriyaki marinade
1 shallot, sliced
¾-inch/2-cm piece fresh ginger,
    finely chopped
2 carrots, sliced
4 oz/115 g button mushrooms,
    sliced
5 cups vegetable stock
9 oz/250 g dried medium
    egg noodles
1 cup frozen peas
6 oz/175 g Chinese cabbage,
    shredded
4 scallions, sliced

method

1 Arrange the salmon fillets, skin-side up, in a dish just large enough to fit them in a single layer. Mix the teriyaki marinade with the shallot and ginger in a small bowl and pour over the salmon. Cover with plastic wrap and let marinate in the refrigerator for at least 1 hour, turning halfway through the marinating time.

2 Put the carrots, mushrooms, and stock into a large pan. Arrange the salmon, skin-side down, on a shallow baking sheet. Pour the fish marinade into the pan of vegetables and stock and bring to a boil. Reduce the heat, cover, and let simmer for 10 minutes.

3 Meanwhile, preheat the broiler to medium. Cook the salmon for 10–15 minutes, depending on the thickness of the fillets, until the flesh flakes easily. Remove from the broiler and keep warm.

4 Add the noodles and peas to the stock and return to a boil. Reduce the heat, cover, and let simmer for 5 minutes, or until the noodles are tender. Stir in the cabbage and scallions and heat through for 1 minute. Divide the noodles and vegetables between 4 warmed serving bowls and top each with a salmon fillet. Serve immediately.

swordfish steaks with lemon dressing

ingredients

serves 4

5 tbsp olive oil,
    plus extra for brushing
juice of ½ large or 1 small lemon
2 garlic cloves, well crushed
2 tsp finely chopped fresh oregano
2 tbsp chopped fresh parsley
4 swordfish steaks, about
    6 oz/175 g each
salt and pepper
lemon wedges, to garnish
freshly cooked asparagus,
    to serve

method

1 Put the oil, lemon juice, garlic and herbs with a little s
and pepper to taste, in a screw-top jar and shake well
to combine.

2 Preheat a ridged broiler pan over high heat. Pat the
swordfish steaks dry with paper towels and lightly
brush with oil on both sides. When the broiler pan
is very hot, add the swordfish steaks and cook for
2 minutes on each side, or until cooked through but
still moist inside.

3 Serve immediately, accompanied by freshly cooked
asparagus and garnished with lemon wedges. Shake
the lemon dressing again and drizzle it over the fish.

lemon & parsley crusted monkfish

ingredients

serves 4

4 tbsp sunflower oil
   or melted butter
4 tbsp fresh breadcrumbs
4 tbsp chopped fresh parsley
finely grated rind of 1 large lemon
4 monkfish fillets, about
   5–6 oz/140–175 g
salt and pepper
fresh sprigs of parsley, to garnish
4 potatoes, peeled, diced,
   and deep-fried, to serve
   (optional)

method

1 Preheat the oven to 350°F/180°C.

2 Mix the oil, breadcrumbs, parsley, and lemon rind with a sprinkling of salt and pepper together in a bowl to give a smooth mixture.

3 Place the fish fillets on a large roasting tray. Divide the breadcrumb mixture between them and press it down carefully onto the fish with your fingers to ensure it covers the fillets.

4 Bake in the oven for 7–8 minutes, or until the fish is cooked. Garnish with fresh sprigs of parsley, and serve with deep-fried potato cubes, if wanted.

fish sticks with chili mayonnaise

ingredients

serves 4

scant 1½ cups all-purpose flour
3 eggs
heaping 1 cup matzo meal
1 lb/450 g firm white fish,
    such as monkfish,
    cut into strips
sunflower or peanut oil,
    for frying
salt and pepper

chili mayonnaise

2 tbsp sweet chili sauce
4–5 tbsp mayonnaise

method

1 Mix the flour with plenty of salt and pepper on a larg
   flat plate. Beat the eggs in a bowl and spread the ma
   meal out on another flat plate.

2 Dip the fish pieces into the seasoned flour, then into
   the beaten egg, then into the matzo meal, ensuring
   generous coating.

3 Pour the oil into a nonstick or heavy skillet to give a
   depth of ½ inch/1 cm, and then heat it up. Cook the
   fish pieces in batches for a few minutes, turning onc
   until golden and cooked through.

4 To make the chili mayonnaise, beat the chili sauce
   and mayonnaise together in a bowl until combined.

5 Transfer the fish to warmed plates or glasses and ser
   with the chili mayonnaise on the side.

seafood kabobs

ingredients

serves 2–4

1 lb/450 g skinless, boneless fish,
   such as monkfish, swordfish,
   and halibut
1 lemon, cut into 8 wedges
8 bay leaves
3 tbsp olive oil

method

1 If you are using wooden skewers, soak them in cold water for at least 30 minutes before using to prevent them from burning.

2 Cut the fish into cubes and thread onto the skewers alternately with the lemon and bay leaves.

3 Preheat the broiler to medium–hot. Brush the kabob with oil and broil for about 4 minutes on each side until the fish is cooked. Serve immediately.

spicy tuna fishcakes

ingredients

serves 4

4 tbsp all-purpose flour
7 oz/200 g canned tuna in oil,
    drained
2–3 tbsp curry paste
1 scallion, trimmed
    and finely chopped
1 egg, beaten
sunflower or peanut oil,
    for frying
salt and pepper
arugula leaves, to serve

method

1 Mix the flour with plenty of salt and pepper on a large flat plate.

2 Mash the tuna with the curry paste, scallion, and beaten egg in a large bowl. Form into 4 fishcakes and dust in the seasoned flour.

3 Heat the oil in a skillet, add the fishcakes, and fry for 3–4 minutes on each side until crisp and golden. Serve on a bed of arugula leaves.

lentil & tuna salad

ingredients

serves 4

1 small red onion, finely chopped

2 ripe tomatoes, seeded and finely chopped

14 oz/400 g canned lentils, drained

6½ oz/185 g canned tuna, drained

2 tbsp chopped fresh cilantro

pepper

dressing

3 tbsp virgin olive oil

1 tbsp lemon juice

1 tsp wholegrain mustard

1 garlic clove, crushed

½ tsp ground cumin

½ tsp ground coriander

method

1 To make the dressing, whisk together the virgin olive oil, lemon juice, mustard, garlic, cumin, and ground coriander in a small bowl until thoroughly combined. Set aside until required.

2 Mix together the chopped onion, chopped tomatoes and drained lentils in a large bowl.

3 Flake the tuna with a fork and stir it into the onion, tomato, and lentil mixture. Stir in the chopped fresh cilantro and mix well.

4 Pour the dressing over the lentil and tuna salad and season with pepper to taste. Serve immediately.

vegetarian

provençal frittata

ingredients

serves 2–4

3 tbsp sunflower or olive oil
1 garlic clove, chopped
8 oz/225 g fresh or frozen spinach
handful of cherry tomatoes, halved
6 eggs, whisked
salt and pepper
cherry tomatoes on the vine,
    to serve (optional)

method

1 Heat the oil in a large skillet, add the garlic, and cook for 1 minute then add the spinach and cook for an additional 1 minute until wilted.

2 Season with salt and pepper, add the halved cherry tomatoes to the skillet, and cook for 1 minute.

3 Pour the eggs into the skillet, stirring, and cook for 4–5 minutes until set. Serve hot or cold, cut into wedges, with cherry tomatoes on the vine, if using.

mixed herb omelet

ingredients

serves 1

2 large eggs
2 tbsp milk
3 tbsp butter
1 fresh flat-leaf parsley sprig,
    stem bruised
leaves from 1 fresh flat-leaf
    parsley sprig
1 fresh chervil sprig
2 freshly snipped chives
salt and pepper
fresh salad leaves, to serve

method

1 Break the eggs into a bowl. Add the milk and salt and pepper to taste, and quickly beat until just blended.

2 Heat an 8-inch/20-cm omelet pan or skillet over medium–high heat until very hot and you can feel the heat rising from the surface. Add 2 tablespoons of the butter and use a fork to rub it over the bottom and around the side of the pan as it melts.

3 As soon as the butter stops sizzling, pour in the eggs. Shake the pan forward and backward over the heat and use the fork to stir the eggs around the pan in a circular motion. Do not scrape the bottom of the pan

4 As the omelet begins to set, use the fork to push the cooked egg from the edge toward the center, so that the remaining uncooked egg comes in contact with the hot bottom of the pan. Continue doing this for 3 minutes, or until the omelet looks set on the bottom but is still slightly runny on top.

5 Put the herbs in the center of the omelet. Tilt the pan away from the handle, so that the omelet slides towa the edge of the pan. Use the fork to fold the top half of the omelet over the herbs. Slide the omelet onto a plate, then rub the remaining butter over the top. Serve immediately, accompanied by fresh salad leave

caramel-topped brie

ingredients

serves 4

2 tbsp water
scant 1 cup granulated sugar
1 whole mini Brie cheese
8 oatcakes and 4 handfuls fresh,
    washed white grapes, to serve
    (optional)

method

1 Heat the water and sugar in a pan over low heat until the sugar has dissolved completely.

2 Increase the heat and cook steadily until the sugar is a dark golden color.

3 Remove the pan from the heat then immediately pour over the Brie on a plate and let set. Serve at room temperature and crack the caramel before serving, with oatcakes and fresh grapes, if using.

goat cheese tarts

ingredients

makes 12

butter, for greasing

14 oz/400 g package prepared and rolled puff pastry

all-purpose flour, for dusting

1 egg, beaten

3 tbsp onion relish or tomato relish

3 x 4 oz/115 g goat cheese logs, sliced

olive oil, for drizzling

pepper

method

1 Preheat the oven to 400°F/200°C and grease several baking sheets.

2 Lay the pastry on a lightly floured work surface and cut out as many 3-inch/7.5-cm rounds as possible.

3 Place the circles on the baking sheets and press gent about 1 inch/2.5 cm from the edge of each, with a smaller 2-inch/5-cm dough cutter.

4 Brush the circles with beaten egg and prick with a fo

5 Top each circle with a little relish and a slice of goat cheese. Drizzle with oil and sprinkle over a little black pepper.

6 Bake for 8–10 minutes, or until the pastry is crisp and the cheese is bubbling. Serve warm.

vegetable tartlets

ingredients

makes 12

butter, for greasing
12 ready-baked pastry shells
2 tbsp olive oil
1 red bell pepper, seeded and diced
1 garlic clove, crushed
1 small onion, finely chopped
8 oz/225 g ripe tomatoes, chopped
1 tbsp torn fresh basil
1 tsp fresh or dried thyme
salt and pepper
green salad, to serve

method

1 Preheat the oven to 400°F/200°C and grease several baking sheets.

2 Place the ready-baked pastry shells on the prepared baking sheets.

3 Heat the oil in a skillet, add the bell pepper, garlic, and onion, and cook over high heat for about 3 minutes until soft.

4 Add the tomatoes, herbs, and seasoning and spoon into the pastry shells.

5 Bake in the preheated oven for about 5 minutes, or until the filling is piping hot. Serve warm with a green salad.

tomato pizza

ingredients

serves 4–6

1 ciabatta loaf, sliced
    horizontally or 9-inch/
    23-cm ready-made
    pizza base
fresh basil leaves, torn

tomato topping
$2/3$ cup crushed tomatoes
3 tbsp tomato paste
2 garlic cloves, crushed
pinch each of sugar, salt,
    and pepper
handful of cherry tomatoes

method

1 Preheat the oven to 400°F/200°C.

2 To make the tomato topping, mix the crushed
tomatoes, tomato paste, garlic, sugar, and salt and
pepper together in a bowl. Spread over the ready-
made pizza base and scatter with the cherry tomatoe

3 Bake in the oven for 8–10 minutes until hot and
bubbling. Scatter the pizza with fresh basil leaves
and serve immediately.

variation

Top the tomato mixture with 4 oz/115 g drained
marinated bell peppers from a jar and a few black olives
Season with salt and pepper, scatter with grated
mozzarella and Parmesan cheese, and bake in the oven

garlic & broccoli crostini

ingredients

serves 6

1 lb 2 oz/500 g broccoli,
    cut into small florets
scant ½ cup olive oil
1 small clove garlic, chopped
1–2 red chiles, seeded and
    finely chopped
6 slices country-style bread
salt and pepper

method

1 Preheat the oven to 375°F/190°C.

2 Cook the broccoli in a large saucepan of salted water for 10 minutes, or until just tender. Drain well and set aside.

3 Heat about one third of the oil in a wok or skillet over a high heat, add the garlic and chile and stir-fry for 2 minutes. Add the broccoli, season to taste with salt and pepper and stir-fry for 3–4 minutes until hot and crisp.

4 Meanwhile, drizzle the remaining oil evenly over the bread slices and bake in the preheated oven for 10 minutes, or until crisp and golden.

5 Divide the broccoli mixture between the crostini, add a grinding of pepper, and serve immediately.

quesadillas

ingredients

serves 4

4 tbsp finely chopped fresh
    jalapeño chiles
1 onion, chopped
1 tbsp red wine vinegar
5 tbsp extra virgin olive oil
10½–14 oz/300–400 g
    canned corn
8 soft flour tortillas

method

1 Put the chiles, onion, vinegar, and 4 tablespoons
    of olive oil in a food processor and process until
    finely chopped.

2 Tip into a bowl and stir in the corn.

3 Heat the remaining oil in a skillet, add a tortilla, and
    cook for 1 minute until golden.

4 Spread one eighth of the chili mixture over the tortilla
    and fold over.

5 Cook for 2–3 minutes until golden and the filling is
    heated through. Remove the quesadillas from the
    skillet and keep warm. Repeat with the other tortillas
    and filling. Serve immediately.

felafel burgers

ingredients

serves 4

1 lb 12 oz/800 g of canned chickpeas, drained and rinsed
1 small onion, chopped
zest and juice of 1 lime
2 tsp ground coriander
2 tsp ground cumin
6 tbsp all-purpose flour
4 tbsp olive oil
4 fresh basil sprigs, to garnish
tomato salsa, to serve

method

1 Put the chickpeas, onion, lime rind and juice, and the spices into a food processor and process to a coarse paste.

2 Tip the mixture out onto a clean work surface or cutting board and shape into 4 burgers.

3 Spread the flour out on a large flat plate and use to coat the burgers.

4 Heat the oil in a large skillet, add the burgers, and coo for 2 minutes on each side until crisp. Garnish with basil and serve with tomato salsa.

crispy spring rolls

ingredients

serves 4

2 tbsp vegetable or peanut oil,
plus extra for deep-frying
6 scallions, cut into 2-inch/5-cm
lengths
1 fresh green chile, seeded
and chopped
1 carrot, cut into thin sticks
1 zucchini, cut into thin sticks
½ red bell pepper, seeded and
thinly sliced
4 oz/115 g/¾ cup bean sprouts
4 oz/115 g canned bamboo shoots,
drained and rinsed
3 tbsp Thai soy sauce
1–2 tbsp chili sauce
8 egg roll skins

method

1 Heat the oil in a preheated wok and stir-fry the scallio
and chile for 30 seconds. Add the carrot, zucchini, and
red bell pepper and stir-fry for 1 minute more. Remov
the wok from the heat and stir in the bean sprouts,
bamboo shoots, soy sauce, and chili sauce. Taste and
add more soy sauce or chili sauce if necessary.

2 Place an egg roll skin on a work surface and spoon
some of the vegetable mixture diagonally across the
center. Roll one corner over the filling and flip the side
of the skin over the top to enclose the filling. Continu
to roll up to make an enclosed package. Repeat with
the remaining skins and filling to make 8 egg rolls.

3 Heat the oil for deep-frying in a wok or large skillet
to 350°F/180°C, or until a cube of bread browns in
30 seconds. Deep-fry the egg rolls, 3–4 at a time,
until they are crisp and golden brown. Remove with
a slotted spoon, drain on paper towels while you coo
the remainder, then serve immediately.

filo-wrapped asparagus

ingredients

serves 4

20 asparagus spears
5 sheets filo pastry
lemon wedges, to serve

cheese dip

85 g/3 oz natural cottage
  cheese
1 tbsp lowfat milk
4 scallions, trimmed
  and finely chopped
2 tbsp chopped fresh mixed
  herbs, such as basil,
  mint, and tarragon
pepper

method

1 To make the dip, put the cottage cheese in a bowl and add the milk. Beat until smooth then stir in the scallions, chopped herbs, and pepper to taste. Place in a serving bowl, cover lightly with plastic wrap and let chill in the refrigerator until required.

2 Cut off and discard the woody ends of the asparagus and shave with a vegetable peeler to remove any woody parts from the spears.

3 Preheat the oven to 375°F/190°C.

4 Cut the filo pastry into quarters and place one sheet on a work surface. Brush lightly with water then place a spear at one end. Roll up and place on a large baking sheet. Repeat until all the asparagus spears are wrapped in pastry.

5 Bake for 10–12 minutes, or until the pastry is golden. Serve the spears with lemon wedges and the dip on the side.

asparagus with lemon butter sauce

ingredients

serves 4

1 lb 12 oz/800 g asparagus
    spears, trimmed
1 tbsp olive oil
salt and pepper

lemon butter sauce

juice of ½ lemon
2 tbsp water
½ cup butter, cut into
    cubes
pepper

method

1 Preheat the oven to 400°F/200°C.

2 Lay the asparagus spears out in a single layer on a large baking sheet. Drizzle over the oil, then season to taste with salt and pepper and roast in the preheated oven for 10 minutes, or until just tender.

3 Meanwhile, make the sauce. Pour the lemon juice into a saucepan and add the water. Heat for a minute or so, then slowly add the butter, cube by cube, stirring constantly until it has all been incorporated. Season to taste with pepper and serve immediately with the asparagus.

chinese-style gingered vegetables

ingredients

serves 2

1 tbsp sunflower or
    peanut oil
1-inch/2.5-cm piece fresh ginger,
    peeled and grated
1 onion, thinly sliced
4 oz/115 g frozen green string
    beans, cut into small pieces
1 lb/450 g bag frozen mixed
    vegetables
²/₃ cup water
2 heaping tbsp dark brown sugar
2 tbsp cornstarch
4 tbsp vinegar
4 tbsp soy sauce
1 tsp ground ginger

method

1 Heat the oil in a wok or large skillet, add the grated ginger, and sauté for 1 minute. Remove from the wok or skillet and drain on paper towels.

2 Reduce the heat slightly and add the vegetables and water to the wok.

3 Cover with a lid or foil and cook for 5–6 minutes, or until the vegetables are tender.

4 Mix the sugar, cornstarch, vinegar, soy sauce, and ground ginger together in a bowl. Increase the heat to medium and add the mixture to the vegetables in the wok. Simmer for 1 minute, stirring, until thickened.

5 Return the ginger to the wok and stir to mix well. Heat through for 2 minutes and then serve immediately.

tofu stir-fry

ingredients

serves 4

2 tbsp sunflower or olive oil
12 oz/350 g firm tofu, cubed
8 oz/225 g bok choy,
    coarsely chopped
1 garlic clove, chopped
4 tbsp sweet chili sauce
2 tbsp light soy sauce

method

1 Heat 1 tablespoon of oil in a wok, add the tofu in batches, and stir-fry for 2 to 3 minutes until golden. Remove and set aside.

2 Add the bok choy to the wok and stir-fry for a few seconds until tender and wilted. Remove and set aside

3 Add the remaining oil to the wok, then add the garlic and stir-fry for 30 seconds.

4 Stir in the chili sauce and soy sauce and bring to a bo

5 Return the tofu and bok choy to the wok and toss gently until coated in the sauce. Serve immediately.

variation

Additional vegetables that you can include in the stir-fry include scallions, bean sprouts, cherry tomatoes, and be peppers with cashews.

wilted spinach, yogurt & walnut salad

ingredients

serves 2

1 lb/450 g fresh spinach leaves
1 onion, chopped
1 tbsp olive oil
1 cup plain yogurt
1 garlic clove, finely chopped
2 tbsp chopped toasted walnuts
2–3 tsp chopped fresh mint
salt and pepper
pita bread, to serve

method

1 Put the spinach and onion into a pan, cover, and cook gently for a few minutes until the spinach has wilted.

2 Add the oil and cook for an additional 5 minutes. Season to taste with salt and pepper.

3 Combine the yogurt and garlic in a bowl.

4 Put the spinach and onion into a serving bowl and pour over the yogurt mixture. Scatter over the walnuts and chopped mint and serve with pita bread.

hot tomato & basil salad

ingredients

serves 6

1lb 9 oz/700 g cherry tomatoes
1 garlic clove, crushed
2 tbsp capers, drained and rinsed
1 tsp granulated sugar
4 tbsp olive oil
2 tbsp torn fresh basil

method

1 Preheat the oven to 400°F/200°C.

2 Stir the tomatoes, garlic, capers, and sugar together in a bowl and tip into a roasting pan.

3 Pour over the oil and toss to coat.

4 Cook in the oven for 10 minutes until the tomatoes are hot.

5 Remove from the oven and tip into a heatproof servin bowl. Scatter over the basil and serve immediately.

moroccan carrot & orange salad

ingredients

serves 4

1 lb/450 g carrots, peeled
1 tbsp olive oil
2 tbsp lemon juice
pinch of granulated sugar
2 large oranges, peeled and
    cut into segments
    (reserve any juice)
⅓ cup raisins
1 tsp ground cinnamon
2 tbsp toasted pine nuts

method

1 Grate the carrots into a large bowl.

2 In a separate bowl, combine the oil, lemon juice, sugar and any orange juice reserved from the preparing of the orange segments.

3 Toss the orange segments with the carrots and stir in the raisins and cinnamon.

4 Pour over the dressing and scatter over the pine nuts just before serving.

avocado salad with lime dressing

ingredients

serves 4

2¼ oz/60 g mixed red and green
    lettuce leaves
2¼ oz/60 g wild arugula
4 scallions, finely diced
5 tomatoes, sliced
¼ cup walnuts, toasted
    and chopped
2 avocados
1 tbsp lemon juice

lime dressing

1 tbsp lime juice
1 tsp French mustard
1 tbsp sour cream
1 tbsp chopped fresh parsley
    or cilantro
3 tbsp extra virgin olive oil
pinch of sugar
salt and pepper

method

1 Wash and drain the lettuce and arugula, if necessary.
Shred all the leaves and arrange in the bottom of a
large salad bowl. Add the scallions, tomatoes, and
chopped walnuts.

2 Pit, peel, and thinly slice or dice the avocados. Brush
with the lemon juice to prevent discoloration, then
transfer to the salad bowl. Gently mix together.

3 To make the dressing, put all the dressing ingredients
in a screw-top jar and shake well. Drizzle over the salad
and serve immediately.

greek salad

ingredients

serves 4

4 tomatoes, cut into wedges
1 onion, sliced
½ cucumber, cut into pieces
8 oz/225 g kalamata olives, stoned
8 oz/225 g feta cheese
  (drained weight), cubed
2 tbsp fresh cilantro leaves
fresh flat-leaf parsley sprigs,
  to garnish
pita bread, to serve

dressing

5 tbsp extra virgin olive oil
2 tbsp white wine vinegar
1 tbsp lemon juice
½ tsp sugar
1 tbsp chopped fresh cilantro
salt and pepper

method

1 To make the dressing, place all the dressing ingredien
  with salt and pepper to taste, in a large bowl and mix
  together well.

2 Add the tomatoes, onion, cucumber, olives, cheese,
  and cilantro to the bowl. Toss all the ingredients
  together, then divide among individual serving bowls
  Garnish with parsley sprigs and serve with
  pita bread.

raspberry & feta salad with couscous

ingredients

serves 6

12 oz/350 g couscous
2½ cups boiling chicken stock
  or vegetable stock
12 oz/350 g fresh raspberries
8 oz/225 g feta cheese (drained
  weight), cubed or crumbled
2 zucchini, thinly sliced
4 scallions, diagonally sliced
⅓ cup pine nuts, toasted
small bunch of fresh basil,
  shredded
grated zest of 1 lemon

dressing

1 tbsp white wine vinegar
1 tbsp balsamic vinegar
4 tbsp extra virgin olive oil
juice of 1 lemon
salt and pepper

method

1 Put the couscous in a large, heatproof bowl and pour over the stock. Stir well, then cover and let soak until all the stock has been absorbed.

2 Meanwhile, pick over the raspberries, discarding any that are overripe.

3 Transfer the couscous to a large serving bowl and stir well to break up any lumps. Add the feta cheese, zucchini, scallions, raspberries, and pine nuts. Stir in the shredded basil and lemon zest and gently toss all the ingredients together.

4 Put all the dressing ingredients in a screw-top jar, with salt and pepper to taste, then screw on the lid and shake until well blended. Pour over the salad and serve immediately.

broiled mozzarella with herbed couscous

ingredients

serves 4

1 lb/450 g mozzarella cheese,
cut into ¼-inch/5-mm slices
4 tbsp chili oil

herbed couscous

1¾ cups hot vegetable stock
heaping 1 cup couscous
2 tbsp chopped fresh mixed
herbs
2 tsp lemon juice
1 tbsp olive oil

method

1 Put the cheese slices in a bowl, pour over the chili oil and toss well to coat the cheese.

2 Preheat the broiler to high and line the broiler rack w foil. Place the cheese on the broiler rack and broil for 2–3 minutes on each side until golden.

3 Meanwhile, stir the hot stock into the couscous in a large bowl. Cover and let stand for 5 minutes.

4 Stir the herbs, lemon juice, and olive oil into the couscous. Serve with the broiled mozzarella cheese.

pasta with chicory & walnuts

ingredients

serves 4

3 tbsp olive oil
2 garlic cloves, crushed
3 heads chicory, sliced
1 tbsp runny honey
1 cup walnuts
1 lb/450 g dried penne pasta
salt and pepper

method

1 Heat the oil in a skillet over low heat, then add the garlic and chicory and cook, stirring, for 3–4 minutes, or until the chicory begins to wilt. Stir in the honey and walnuts and cook, stirring occasionally, for an additio 4–5 minutes. Season to taste with salt and pepper.

2 Meanwhile, cook the pasta in a large saucepan of lightly salted boiling water according to the package directions, or until tender but still firm to the bite. Dra and toss with the chicory mixture. Serve immediately

pasta with spicy olive sauce

ingredients

serves 2–4

12 oz/350 g fresh pasta shapes
½ tsp salt, plus extra for
    cooking the pasta
6 tbsp olive oil
½ tsp freshly grated nutmeg
½ tsp pepper
1 garlic clove, crushed
2 tbsp tapenade
½ cup black or green olives,
    pitted and sliced
1 tbsp chopped fresh parsley,
    to garnish

method

1 Cook the pasta in a large pan of boiling salted water for about 4 minutes, or according to the package directions, until tender but still firm to the bite.

2 Meanwhile, put ½ teaspoon of salt with the oil, nutmeg, pepper, garlic, tapenade, and olives in another saucepan and heat slowly but do not allow to boil. Cover and let stand for 3–4 minutes.

3 Drain the pasta and return to the pan. Add the olive sauce and heat gently for 1 to 2 minutes. Serve immediately, garnished with chopped parsley.

mozzarella gnocchi

ingredients

serves 3–4

butter, for greasing
1 lb/450 g package potato gnocchi
scant 1 cup heavy cream
8 oz/225 g firm mozzarella cheese,
    grated or chopped
salt and pepper

method

1 Preheat the broiler and grease a large baking dish.

2 Cook the potato gnocchi in a large pan of boiling salted water for about 3 minutes, or according to the package directions. Drain and put into the prepared baking dish.

2 Season the cream with salt and pepper and drizzle over the gnocchi. Scatter over the cheese and broil for a few minutes until the top is browned and bubbling. Serve immediately.

desserts

nectarine crunch

ingredients

serves 3

4 nectarines
6 oz/175 g raisin and nut
    crunchy oat cereal
1¼ cups lowfat plain yogurt
2 tbsp peach preserve
2 tbsp peach nectar

method

1 Using a sharp knife, cut the nectarines in half, then remove and discard the pits. Chop the flesh into bite-size pieces. Reserve a few pieces for decoration and put a few of the remaining pieces in the bottom of 3 sundae glasses. Put a layer of oat cereal in each glass, then drizzle over a little of the yogurt.

2 Put the preserve and peach nectar in a pitcher and stir together to mix. Add a few more nectarine pieces to the glasses and drizzle over a little of the preserve. Continue building up the layers in this way, finishing with a layer of yogurt and a sprinkling of oat cereal. Decorate with the reserved nectarine pieces and serve.

pan-fried apples or pears with maple syrup & walnuts

ingredients

serves 4

6 tbsp butter

4 firm pears or apples, peeled and cut into thick slices

3 tbsp maple syrup

2 tbsp brandy

4 tbsp walnuts

method

1 Melt half the butter in a skillet and add half the pears or apples.

2 Cook for 2 minutes on each side until golden. Remove from the skillet and cook the remaining fruit, then remove from the skillet.

3 Add the remaining butter to the skillet with the maple syrup, brandy, and walnuts and bring to a boil. Remove from the heat.

4 Put the warm fruit into serving bowls and pour over the sauce. Serve.

fruit skewers

ingredients

serves 4

a selection of fruit, such as apricots,
    peaches, figs, strawberries,
    mangoes, pineapple, bananas,
    dates, and papaya, prepared
    and cut into chunks
2 tbsp maple syrup
1¾oz/50 g semisweet chocolate,
    broken into chunks

method

1 Soak 4 wooden skewers in water for at least 30 minutes
   to prevent them from burning. Thread alternate pieces
   of fruit onto each skewer. Brush the fruit with a little
   maple syrup.

2 Put the chocolate in a heatproof bowl set over a pan
   of gently simmering water, ensuring that the bowl
   does not touch the water, and heat until the chocolate
   has melted.

3 Preheat the broiler to high and line the broiler pan
   with foil. Broil the fruit skewers for 3 minutes, or until
   caramelized. Serve drizzled with the melted chocolate.

broiled tropical fruits with spiced butter

ingredients

serves 4

8 tbsp unsalted butter

2 tbsp chopped preserved ginger

½ tsp ground cinnamon

½ tsp grated nutmeg

2 tsp lemon juice

2 tsp confectioners' sugar

4 bananas, halved

4 pineapple wedges

2 papayas, peeled, seeded and sliced

1 mango, peeled, pitted and sliced

method

1 Cream the butter with the ginger, spices, lemon juice, and confectioners' sugar in a large bowl.

2 Spread half of the spicy butter mixture over the pieces of fruit.

3 Preheat the broiler or barbecue. Place the fruit on the broiler rack and broil for 2–3 minutes until beginning to caramelize.

4 Turn the fruit over, dot with the remaining spiced butter and broil until caramelized. Serve immediately.

orange & caramel bananas

ingredients

serves 4

½ cup granulated
    or superfine sugar
1 tsp vanilla extract
finely grated zest and
    juice of 1 orange
4 bananas, peeled
    and thickly sliced
2 tbsp butter
ice cream, to serve

method

1 Put the sugar, vanilla extract, and orange juice in
   a skillet and heat gently until it forms a caramel.

2 Add the banana slices and cook, shaking the skillet, f
   1 to 2 minutes until they are coated with the carame

3 Add the butter to the skillet and cook for an addition
   3 minutes, shaking the skillet to coat the bananas.

4 Tip the bananas onto a serving plate and sprinkle wit
   the orange zest. Serve hot with scoops of ice cream.

plums in spiced red wine

ingredients

serves 2–4

1¼ cups red wine
3 heaping tbsp dark brown sugar
1 cinnamon stick, broken
4 cardamom pods, cracked
pinch of ground cloves
8 firm red plums, pitted
and halved
4 tbsp sour cream, to serve

method

1 Put the red wine, sugar, cinnamon, cardamom, and ground cloves in a pan and slowly bring to a boil, stirring until the sugar has dissolved completely.

2 Add the plums to the pan and cook gently for about 5 minutes.

3 Remove from the heat and let cool completely before serving with sour cream.

berry brûlées

ingredients

serves 4–6

1 lb/450 g berries, such as
   raspberries, strawberries,
   and pitted cherries
1¼ cups heavy cream
½ cup superfine sugar

method

1 Divide the berries among 4–6 individual ovenproof
   dishes or one large dish.

2 Whip the cream in a large bowl until thick but not stiff.

3 Spoon the whipped cream over the berries until they
   are evenly covered.

4 Preheat the broiler to very hot. Sprinkle over the
   sugar to cover the cream completely and place under
   the broiler, about 2–3 inches/5–7.5 cm from the heat
   source, for about 3 minutes, or until the sugar is
   bubbling and golden. Watch the sugar carefully
   because it will scorch if left too long.

cherry mascarpone creams

ingredients

serves 4

15 oz/425 g canned black cherries
    in syrup, pitted
1 tbsp rose water
2½ cups mascarpone cheese
slivered toasted almonds or
    chopped pistachios,
    to decorate

method

1 Drain the pitted cherries and set aside 2 tablespoons of the syrup.

2 Stir the rose water into the reserved cherry syrup, then stir into the cherries.

3 Spoon into 4 serving dishes. Cover the cherries with the mascarpone and sprinkle with the almonds or pistachios. Let chill in the refrigerator until ready to serve.

white wine & honey dessert

ingredients

serves 4–6

3 tbsp brandy

3 tbsp white wine

2½ cups heavy cream

6 tbsp honey

½ cup slivered almonds

method

1 Combine the brandy and white wine in a bowl.

2 Whip the cream in a large bowl until just thickened.

3 Add the honey to the cream and whip again for about 15 seconds.

4 Pour the brandy and wine mixture in a continuous stream onto the cream and honey mixture, whisking continuously until all the liquid is absorbed and the mixture forms soft peaks.

5 Spoon into serving dishes and let chill in the refrigerator for 2 to 3 hours.

6 Just before serving, scatter over the almonds.

mocha puddings

ingredients

serves 2–4

12 marshmallows
½ cup strong black coffee
2 oz/55 g semisweet chocolate,
    finely chopped or grated
1¼ cups heavy cream

method

1 Put the marshmallows in a pan with the coffee and ha
   the chocolate. Heat gently until melted. Remove the
   pan from the heat.

2 Whip the cream in a large bowl until thick and softly
   peaking, then gently stir in the coffee mixture.

3 Spoon into 2–4 serving bowls or dishes and sprinkle
   with the remaining chocolate. Let chill in the
   refrigerator until ready to serve.

brown sugar mocha cream dessert

ingredients

serves 4–6

1¼ cups heavy cream
1 tsp vanilla extract
1¾ cups fresh whole wheat
    breadcrumbs
scant ½ cup dark brown sugar
1 tbsp instant coffee granules
2 tbsp unsweetened cocoa
grated chocolate, to decorate

method

1 Whip the cream and vanilla extract together in a large bowl until thick and softly peaking.

2 Mix the breadcrumbs, sugar, coffee, and cocoa together in another large bowl. Layer the breadcrumb mixture with the whipped cream in serving glasses, ending with a layer of whipped cream. Sprinkle with grated chocolate.

3 Cover tightly with plastic wrap and let chill in the refrigerator until ready to serve.

jamaican parfait

ingredients

serves 2

1¼ cups heavy cream
2 tbsp light brown sugar
1 tbsp strong coffee or coffee
    liqueur
2 tbsp dark rum
2 ripe bananas
chocolate-covered coffee beans,
    to decorate

method

1 Whip the cream, sugar, and coffee together in a large bowl until thick and softly peaking.

2 Gradually fold in the rum.

3 Peel and slice the bananas, then gently stir into the cream mixture.

4 Spoon into serving glasses or bowls and top with chocolate-covered coffee beans. Let chill until ready to serve.

cheat's chocolate pots

ingredients

serves 4–6

5 oz/140 g good-quality
semisweet chocolate, broken
into small pieces or chopped
1¾ cups heavy cream
1 tsp vanilla extract

method

1 Melt the chocolate in a bowl set over a pan of simmering, not boiling, water, or melt in a glass or ceramic bowl in a microwave oven.

2 Remove the bowl from the pan or microwave and gradually stir in the cream and vanilla extract until the mixture is smooth.

3 Pour into small coffee cups or dishes and let chill in the refrigerator until ready to serve.

chocolate zabaglione

ingredients

serves 4

4 egg yolks
⅓ cup superfine sugar
5 tbsp Marsala
unsweetened cocoa, for dusting
amaretti cookies, to serve

method

1 Whisk the egg yolks with the sugar in a heatproof bowl or, if you have one, the top of a double boiler for about 1 minute.

2 Gently whisk in the Marsala. Set the bowl over a pan of barely simmering water or put the top of the double boiler on its bottom filled with barely simmering water and whisk vigorously for 10–15 minutes, until thick, creamy and foamy.

3 Spoon the hot mixture into warmed coffee cups and dust with cocoa powder. Serve the zabaglione as soon as possible so that it is warm, light and fluffy, accompanied by crunchy amaretti cookies.

no-bake chocolate fudge cake

ingredients
serves 6-8

8 oz/225 g semisweet chocolate,
   broken into pieces
1 cup unsalted butter
3 tbsp black coffee
¼ cup light brown sugar
few drops of vanilla extract
8 oz/225 g graham crackers,
   crushed
½ cup raisins
¾ cup walnuts, chopped

method

1 Line a 1-lb/450-g loaf pan or an 8-inch/20-cm round cake pan with wax paper or nonstick parchment paper. Melt the chocolate, butter, coffee, sugar, and vanilla extract in a pan over low heat.

2 Add the crushed crackers, raisins, and walnuts and stir well.

3 Spoon the mixture into the prepared loaf pan.

4 Let the mixture set, then chill in the refrigerator for 1–2 hours. Turn out and cut into thin slices to serve.

ginger baked alaskas

ingredients

serves 4

4 tbsp golden raisins or raisins
3 tbsp dark rum or ginger wine
4 square slices ginger cake
4 scoops vanilla ice cream or rum
    and raisin ice cream
3 egg whites
scant 1 cup granulated
    or superfine sugar

method

1 Preheat the oven to 450°F/230°C.

2 Mix the golden raisins with the rum in a small bowl.

3 Place the cake slices well apart on a baking sheet and scatter a spoonful of the soaked golden raisins on each slice.

4 Place a scoop of ice cream in the center of each slice and place in the freezer.

5 Meanwhile, whisk the egg whites in a large grease-free bowl until soft peaks form then gradually whisk the sugar into the egg whites, a tablespoonful at a time, until the mixture forms stiff peaks.

6 Remove the ice cream-topped cake slices from the freezer and spoon the meringue mixture over the ice cream. Spread to cover the ice cream completely.

7 Bake in the oven for about 5 minutes until starting to brown. Serve immediately.

chocolate banana sundae

ingredients

serves 4

⅔ cup heavy cream
4 bananas, peeled
8 scoops vanilla ice cream
¾ cup chopped mixed nuts, toasted
1½ oz/40 g milk or semisweet
    chocolate, grated
4 ice cream fan-shape wafers,
    to serve

chocolate sauce
2 oz/55 g semisweet chocolate
4 tbsp dark corn syrup
1 tbsp butter
1 tbsp cognac or dark rum
    (optional)

method

1 To make the chocolate sauce, break the chocolate into small pieces and place in a heatproof bowl with the corn syrup and butter. Set over a pan of gently simmering water until melted, stirring until well combined. Remove the bowl from the heat and stir in the cognac, if using.

2 Whip the cream until just holding its shape, and slice the bananas. Place a scoop of ice cream in the bottom of each of 4 sundae glasses. Top with slices of banana, some chocolate sauce, a spoonful of cream, and a generous sprinkling of nuts.

3 Repeat the layers, finishing with a good dollop of whipped cream, a sprinkling of nuts and a little grated chocolate. Serve with fan wafers.

index